The Complete
Slow Cooker
Recipe Book

Quick, Easy and Delicious Recipes for Every Day
incl. Keto Diet and Low Carb Recipes

[1st Edition]

Betty K. Harris

ISBN - 9781697600513

Table of contents

Introduction

Entertaining using a slow cooker allows you to throw a few handfuls of ingredients in, climb back into bed to wake up hours later, invite your mates inside and pretend you slaved over the preparation. No one will know you slept the day away instead....

There are no words to fully describe the satisfaction of coming home after a testing day out in the world, to find a perfectly prepared meal waiting for you. Hot and tasty and ready to eat! And made by you while you were out living life and experiencing the world outside your kitchen. This is the joy of having a slow cooker of your very own.

If you're still indecisive about the wisdom of owning this magical uni-corn of the cooking world, read on... the benefits extent even further than effective time management to cost effectiveness. The slow cooker is perfect for making a meal fit for a king from 'peasant' cuts of meat, dry goods in your grocery pantry, and any and every conceivable vegetable. Depending on the particular slow cooker, most offer a minimum of two cooking temperatures. Setting the cooker at LOW (140°C-160°C/280°F -320°F), before you set off in the morning will magically provide you and yours with that promised hot and tasty evening meal when you are good and ready for it. And all this without the need for overseeing, stirring, adding or adjusting.

Using Your Slow Cooker

While the cooker does it all for you, you may have to put in just a little planning to get the most benefit. It is true that food should be at room temp when put on to cook, but you can nonetheless pre-prepare the night before. Simply pile all the necessary ingredients into slow cooker dish, pop it into the fridge overnight, and then remove it at least a half hour before placing it into the cooker base. For recipes requiring ingredients to be placed into the cooker dish when it is already warm, just have the ingredients already ready and waiting in a separate container suitable for refrigeration.

Which one is best?

First, you will need to select just the right magical slow cooker for your needs.

Size

Size does in fact count when choosing a slow cooker that fits your specific requirements. Simply put, you could go according to the number of persons you will be catering for. Just remember that you may be cooking only for yourself most of the time, but what about those occasions when you will want to be entertaining? Bigger may be better even for a single person or a couple, since leftovers can be easily frozen or refrigerated for a separate meal. Everyone knows that a curry always tastes better when it is dished up some time after it is freshly prepared. Also bear in mind that a slow cooker tends to be at its best when filled around half way.

1 person: 1½ to 3-½ quart (2 litre)

2 people: 2 to 3½ quart (3 litre)

3 to 4 people: 3-½ to 4-½ quart (3.5 litre)

4 to 5 people: 4-½ to 5 quart (4.5 litre)

Party sizes are also available. Check them out if you need the big guns!

Price

Prices range according to the features of the different models. Do not be too dauted by price. Very few people need more than a cooker that uses its unique environment to heat food slowly and steadily without the risk of cooking dry or burning. Convenient features that come at a price are available if you feel you would prefer the extras.

Temperature Controls

Gone are the days when slow cookers allowed only two options: HIGH and LOW, which had to be manually operated. Modern slow cookers offer the convenience of a 'Keep Warm' feature, which is great when keeping a meal at ready-to-eat temperatures after it has cooked but it's not quite time for serving yet. Further to this though, you can now choose between a manual or digital slow cooker. Manual slow cookers will require you turn the cooker on and off as required. Slow cookers with the digital programming feature can be set to turn on, turn off, schedule the number of hours to cook, and even revert to 'Warm' at a predetermined time.

As with everything, there are pros and cons to both the manual and digital options. A power failure, for example, will render the digital slow cooker ineffectual. It will simply turn off and not resume cooking until it is manually turned on again. A manual slow cooker will turn back on as before when the power supply resumes. Manual options are always simpler to use, but then again, they lack the convenience of a digital option.

Shape

Slow cookers are available in various shapes: round, oval, oblong or rectangular. Oval seems the most preferred option as it allows for an easy fit for a whole bird, roasts, and most meat cuts.

Crock and Lid

A removable dish is preferable, making the slow cooker easy to clean, and serving as a convenient serving dish. Glass lids are best since they allow for checking the contents of the dish without removing the lids. Removing the lid during cooking may lead to a longer cooking time since much heat is lost in this exercise.

Tips & Tricks

- Select the right size cooker for your needs

- Start off by cooking a dish you know well until you have the confidence to jump in the 'deep end' with slow-cooking new dishes and recipes

- Brown meat before adding to your slow cooker. Trim excess fat from meat before browning

- Remove chicken skin from chicken thighs before browning

- Avoid the temptation to lift the lid off the cooker while it is preparing your meal. This reduces the cooking temperature and may affect the moisture content, also possibly lengthening the cooking time

- Always place the cooker dish in the cooker base before heating the cooker base. Do not put the dish into a pre-heated cooker base unless the recipe specifically calls for this, in which case make sure that the cooker dish is at room temperature

- Never place a refrigerated cooker dish into the cooker base. Always bring it up to room temperature before placing in the cooker base

- Do not immerse the hot dish or lid in cold water or fill it with cold water when hot

- Slow cookers operate such that they do not allow for much evaporation of liquids. Try to use recipes especially formulated for slow cookers. When using a conventional recipe, adapt the liquid content accordingly. A good rule of thumb is to minimise the liquid amount stipulated by a third

- Season sparingly during cooking, opting to adjust the flavour according to taste before serving

- To add zest to a dish, splash a squeeze of lemon juice, sprinkle in fresh herbs for extra flavour, or use your discretion according to the type of dish you are preparing.

Cleaning Your Slow Cooker

The best advice is to check the manual for your slow cooker for washing instructions. Some slow cookers can be put into a dishwasher, which is great. Whatever your model requires, it is always advisable to clean the slow cooker dish and base as soon as possible after use. Better still is to prevent the slow cooker from staining by spraying it with a non-stick cooking spray, and never overfilling the cooker dish. Stubborn stains need extra work, and here are some tips:

· Leave the slow cooker to cook the stain off by filling the cooker dish with water to just above the stain or ring, and leaving it to cook for an hour or two

To clean the casing itself, some care should be taken:

· Always unplug the unit before washing and never immerse the base in water

- Wipe clean with a soft cloth, dampened and with dishwashing detergent
- More stubborn marks may need a mixture of fresh lemon juice or vinegar and baking soda applied with a sponge, and wiped off
- Do not use abrasive cleaners or harsh detergents

Watch out for....

Convenience does not get any better than bringing a slow cooker into your life but watch out for....

- When preparing in advance, store meat separately from other ingredients, especially fresh vegetables
- Meat and vegetables should ideally be prepared on separate cutting boards
- Reheating leftovers in the slow cooker is a no-no! Rather opt for the microwave oven or conventional cooker to reheat
- Bacteria may get access to your food if you allow it to stand in the slow cooker for too long without refrigeration or optimum heating
- When adding browned meat to the slow cooker, always add the morsels remaining in the pan to be sure you include the added flavour that goes with the browned meat. Work these browned

bits loose even more effectively by cooking it loose in the browning pan through deglazing with wine, water or stock

- Only use wine for cooking that you would opt to drink, especially a dry wine

- Those in the know crumble ginger bread cookies into pot roast and beef stew cooked in the slow cooker, for added flavour and improved texture.

RECIPES FOR BREAKFAST

French Toast

Time: 3hrs 10 minutes | Serves 8

Ingredients:

♦ 10½ slices French bread, torn

♦ 8 eggs

♦ ⅓ cup brown sugar or honey

♦ 2 cups milk

♦ 1⅓ tsp vanilla

♦ 3 tsp cinnamon

Preparation:

1. Spray 2 litre (2.5-4 quart) slow cooker dish with non-stick spray. Place shredded bread inside

2. Whisk together eggs, milk, sugar, cinnamon and vanilla. Pour mix over bread cubes, pressing down with spatula so that bread becomes soaked through

3. Cook for 3 or 4 hrs on LOW OR on HIGH for 1½ to 2 hrs. French toast should be set in the centre and not gooey. Serve hot with honey, fresh fruit, berry compote or to taste.

Brekkie Casserole Overnighter

Time: 7 to 8 hours | Serves up to 8

Ingredients:

- Non-stick cooking spray
- 12 eggs
- 1 cup milk
- 240ml (8oz) sour cream
- 2 tsp Dijon mustard
- 2 cups shredded potatoes, frozen
- 250g (8oz) deli ham, diced sliced 13mm thick (½-inch)
- Bell pepper, cored, seeded, & chopped
- 2 cups baby spinach (2oz)
- 1 chopped red onion
- 1½ cups cheddar cheese, grated, divided
- Salt and ground black pepper

Preparation:

1. Spray large size slow cooker with non-stick cooking spray

2. Whisk together eggs, milk, sour cream, mustard, salt, and pepper. Stir in potatoes, ham, peppers, onion, spinach, and 1 cup of cheese. Combine and smooth to an even layer. Cover

3. Cook on LOW for 7 to 8hrs, until eggs are lightly browned at the edges and cooked through. Turn slow cooker off. Sprinkle ½ cup cheese on top, cover for 5 min, until cheese is melted.

Overnight Oats with Cinnamon Apple

Time: 5 hrs 15 min | Serves 8

Ingredients:

- 1 cup oats
- 1 ½ cups coconut milk
- 2 diced apples, peeled, cored
- 1 ½ cups water
- 2 tbsp brown sugar
- 1 tsp cinnamon
- 1 tbsp coconut oil
- Sea salt

Preparation:

1. Thoroughly coat the cooker dish with non-stick cooking spray
2. Add all the ingredients to the slow cooker. Stir well to combine
3. Cook on LOW for 5 to 7hrs according to your slow cooker
4. Serve with desired toppings: honey/fresh fruit/nuts

Brekkie Strata

Serves 6

Ingredients:

- Non-stick cooking spray
- 7 cups French loaf, cubed, dried out at room temperature on an uncovered tray
- 170 to 225g (6 to 8 oz) chicken breakfast sausage, out of casing
- 2 tbsp canola oil
- Diced red bell pepper
- Chopped white onion
- 1 clove grated garlic
- Salt and pepper
- 8 large eggs
- 1 ½ cups (6 oz) grated cheese
- 2 cups cream

Preparation:

1. Coat the cooker dish well with non-stick spray

2. Heat oil and cook sausage, breaking it into pieces. Brown for approx. 5 mins, remove from heat and set one side

3. Cook bell pepper, onion, garlic, salt and pepper to taste in hot oil, stirring occasionally for 8 mins, until soft but not browned. Remove from heat and add sausage

4. Whisk eggs and cream with salt and pepper to taste

5. Layer slow cooker with half the bread, sprinkle ½ cup cheese over and add remaining bread. Layer sausage and veg mix on top and then cover it all with egg mixture and remaining cup of cheese. Cover. Cook on LOW for 4 hrs. Cool a little before removing and serving in wedges.

Cheesy Bacon Layers

Time: 4 hrs15 mins | Serves 10

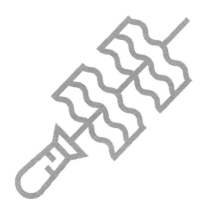

Ingredients:

- 10 eggs
- 125g (8 oz) Cheddar Cheese
- 2½ cups milk
- 16 slices toasted and cubed French bread, 19mm thick (¾ inch)
- 10 rashers bacon, cooked and crumbled
- 4 green onions
- Salt and Pepper

Preparation:

1. Whisk eggs, milk and pepper together and add all ingredients, retaining just ½ cup cheese. Mix well

2. Line slow cooker with foil strips along bottom and sides, and spray with non-stick cooking spray. Pour in the egg mixture, pressing toast cubes in with back of spoon to moisten them

3. Cook on LOW for 4 hrs. Sprinkle remaining cheese over during the final 15 min of cooking. Cool a little before removing the foil and strata from the cooker.

Mexican Breakfast

Time: 4hrs 30 minutes | Serves 8

Ingredients:

- 451g (1 lb) chorizo, cooked
- 8 eggs
- 9 corn tortillas
- 1½ cups milk
- 1 chopped seeded jalapeño chile
- ¾ cup sliced green onions
- 1 chopped red bell pepper
- 2 tbsp chopped fresh cilantro
- 2 cups grated cheese
- 1 cup chunky salsa

Preparation:

1. Spray 5 litre (6 quart) slow cooker dish with non-stick spray. Arrange 3 tortillas to cover bottom

2. Whisk eggs, chile and milk. Keep one side. Add 2 tbsp chopped bell pepper, 2 tbsp onions and ¾ cup cheese

3. Add half the chorizo, the bell pepper, onions and cheese not kept one side, in layers on the tortillas in the dish. Repeat, topping with the remaining 3 tortillas, covering the mixture. Cover tortillas with egg mixture. Cover and cook to set in centre, on LOW for 4 to 5hrs OR on HIGH for 2 to 3 hrs

4. Sprinkle the reserved cheese, bell pepper and onions over together with cilantro. Remove foil, loosen edges with blunt knife and serve.

Granola

Time: varies | 5 cups

Ingredients:

- Non-stick cooking spray
- 4 cups rolled oats
- 1 cup raw nuts (almonds/walnuts/pecans) and seeds
- ½ tsp ground cinnamon
- ¼ cup brown sugar
- ½ tsp salt
- ½ cup olive/coconut oil
- ½ cup honey/maple syrup
- ½ cup dried fruit
- 1 tbsp vanilla extract

Preparation:

1. Spray inside of slow cooker with non-stick cooking spray

2. Add all the dry ingredients and stir. Add wet ingredients, stirring until dry ingredients are coated well

3. Cook granola on HIGH for 2 to 2½ hrs, with lid slightly askew so that moisture can escape to ensure a crunchy granola. Stir every 30 mins, cooking until golden and toasted

4. Turn off slow cooker and stir in dried fruit. Cool completely or spread over sheet, and store in airtight container at room temp.

Summer Fruit Sauce

Time: Varies | Makes 5 cups

Ingredients:

- 6 cups mixed summer fruit, washed, dried, pitted/stoned and cut into bite size pieces
- 1 cup water
- ½ cup sugar
- 1 vanilla bean, split lengthwise

Preparation:

1. Combine all ingredients in slow cooker. Cover

2. Cook, depending on the fruit until the fruit is softened and of a sauce consistency. For berries, 2 to 3 hrs on HIGH; stone fruit, rhubarb, and cherries on HIGH 3 to 4 hrs

3. Remove vanilla bean and serve the sauce warm over pancakes, waffles, cooked oats, or French toast.

Breakfast Frittata

Time: 3hrs 5 mins | Serves 6

Ingredients:

♦ Non-stick cooking spray

♦ ¾ cups spinach, frozen

♦ ½ cup red bell pepper

♦ ¼ cup diced red onion

♦ 8 eggs, beaten

♦ Salt and Black Pepper

♦ 1⅓ cups breakfast sausage

Preparation:

1. Line slow cooker well with non-stick cooking spray, and add the frozen spinach, red pepper, red onions, eggs, sausage, salt & pepper

2. Cook on LOW for 2 to 3 hrs until frittata is set.

English Breakfast

Time: 3 to 4 hrs| Serves 6

Ingredients:

- ◆ 6 sausages
- ◆ 6 rashers bacon
- ◆ 1 can baked beans
- ◆ 1 can chopped tomatoes or plum tomatoes
- ◆ 50g (2oz) mushrooms, quartered
- ◆ 4 eggs
- ◆ 15g (½-oz) butter

Preparation:

1. Measure out baked beans, tomatoes, eggs, mushrooms equally in separate mugs

2. Beat eggs with fork, season with salt and pepper, add 8g butter. Add remaining butter to the mushrooms

3. Put the mugs in the middle with sausages placed around the sides, with rolled up bacon rashers

4. Cook on HIGH for 3 to 4 hrs. Serve with buttered toast as preferred.

RECIPES FOR MAIN DISHES

BEEF MAIN DISHES

Beef Pot Roast

Time: 7 hrs 30 minutes | Serves 6 - 8

Ingredients:

- 1½ kg (3.3lb) rolled beef brisket
- 2 tbsp flour
- 2 tbsp sunflower oil
- 3 chopped carrots
- 3 chopped celery sticks
- 2 chopped parsnips
- 1 onion, chopped
- 80g (2.85oz) button mushrooms
- 2 tsp English mustard
- 2 bay leaves
- 2 crushed garlic cloves
- 500ml (17oz) red wine
- 250ml (8½ oz) beef stock

Preparation:

1. Thoroughly cover beef brisket in 2 tbsp flour seasoned with salt and pepper. Meanwhile heat 3 tbsp sunflower oil and sear the meat on all sides

2. Put carrots, celery, onion, parsnips, and mushrooms in slow cooker and place seared beef on top. Add bay leaves, garlic, English mustard, followed by wine and stock. Cover and cook for 7 hrs on LOW

3. Preheat oven to 201°C (390°F). Remove beef from slow cooker, arrange on greased baking tray, and oven roast for 20 mins. Meanwhile, ladle liquid from slow cooker into shallow pan and reduce to rich gravy by boiling at high heat

4. Slice and serve with the prepared veg, roast potatoes, and gravy.

Beef Goulash

Time: 7 hrs | Serves 8

Ingredients:

- 3 tbsp olive oil
- 3 crushed garlic cloves
- 2kg (4.4lbs) stewing steak, into chunks
- 2 onions finely chopped
- 4 mixed peppers, diced to 4cm (1.6 inches)
- 2 tbsp flour
- 2 tsp caraway seeds | 2 tsp hot smoked paprika
- 1 tbsp sweet smoked paprika
- 400 to 500ml (13½–17 oz) beef stock
- 4 tbsp tomato purée | 4 tomatoes, in chunks
- 300ml (10oz) soured cream | chopped parsley

Preparation:

1. Heat 2 tbsp oil and sear the seasoned beef in batches, browning all sides. Set one side on a plate

2. Add remaining oil and fry onions until lightly golden for 10 mins. Add peppers and garlic, and fry for further 5 to 10 mins. Add flour and spices. Stir and cook for 2 mins. Add tomatoes, tomato purée, and 400ml beef stock. Stir, season and simmer

3. Add the simmering liquid to the seared beef in slow cooker, covering the meat if necessary using the remaining stock. Cover and cook on LOW, 6 to 7 hrs – removing when sauce has thickened adequately

4. Season, swirl in soured cream and parsley and sprinkle remaining parsley and sweet smoked paprika over top

5. Serve with small roasted potatoes/rice, as preferred.

Beef Ragu

Time: 6 hrs15 minutes | Serves 8

Ingredients:

- 1 tsp olive oil
- 6 slightly smashed garlic cloves
- 700g (1½ lbs) flank steak, quartered and cut against grain
- salt and black pepper
- ¼ cup beef stock/ dry red wine
- 1 can (28 oz) crushed tomatoes
- 2 bay leaves

- 1 finely chopped carrot
- 2 sprigs fresh thyme
- 450g (16 oz) pasta
- To serve:
- ½ cup Parmesan cheess, freshly-grated
- ½ cup ricotta cheese
- Garnish with chopped fresh parsley

Preparation:

1. Cook garlic in heated oil, stirring for 2 mins
2. Season beef to taste and cook in slow cooker, adding first the tomatoes and broth and then garlic, carrots, bay leaves, thyme. Cover and cook on LOW for 8 to 10 hrs OR on HIGH for 6 hrs. Discard herbs. Shred beef while in cooker dish, using 2 forks
3. Cook pasta, drain and put back in pot, adding the sauce from the slow cooker. Cook for 1 min, stirring to combine pasta and sauce

Roast Beef

Time: 1 hr 40 minutes | Serves 12

Ingredients:

♦ 2.3kg (5 lbs) chuck roast
♦ Salt and ground black pepper
♦ 2 cloves garlic, grated
♦ 1 tbsp canola oil

Preparation:

1. Rub roast with garlic, salt, & pepper. Heat canola oil and sear beef for 3 to 4 mins. Relocate beef and drippings to slow cooker. Cook on LOW for 90 mins

2. Check that beef is roasted to ideal preference. Remove and serve or cook a little longer until done to preference.

Beef Bourguignon

Time: 9 hrs 20 minutes | Serves 6

Ingredients:

- 5 finely chopped rashers bacon,
- 1.4kg (3 lbs) boneless chuck, cubed to 2½ cm (1 inch)
- 1 cup red cooking wine
- ¼ cup soy sauce
- ½ cup tomato sauce
- ¼ cup flour
- 3 garlic cloves, finely chopped
- 2 tbsp finely chopped thyme
- 5 Carrots, sliced
- 500g (1lb) baby potatoes
- 230g s(8 oz) sliced mushrooms
- 2 cups chicken broth
- Garnish with chopped parsley

Preparation:

1. Crisp bacon in skillet. Remove to slow cooker. Sear seasoned beef in the same skillet for 2 to 4min. Add seared beef to slow cooker.

2. Deglaze skillet using red wine, scraping browned bits off side. Simmer and reduce. Add tomato sauce. Chicken broth, and soy sauce slowly, and whisk in flour. Add to slow cooker

3. Add garlic, thyme, carrots, potatoes, and mushrooms. Stir and cook on LOW for 8 to 10 hrs OR HIGH for 6hrs.

Beef Stew

Time: 8hrs 50 minutes | Serve 8

Ingredients:

- 900g (2 lb) stewing beef, cubed
- 2 tbsp olive oil
- Salt & ground black pepper
- 3 minced cloves garlic
- 4 carrots, sliced diagonally
- 1 diced onion
- 450g (1 lb) baby potatoes, quartered
- 2 tbsp tomato paste
- 3 cups beef broth
- ¼ cup flour
- 1 tbsp Worcestershire sauce
- 1 tsp dried thyme | 1 tsp dried rosemary
- 1 tsp caraway seeds | 1 tsp smoked paprika
- 2 bay leaves
- 2 tbsp chopped fresh parsley

Preparation:

1. Brown seasoned beef for 2 to 3 mins in hot olive oil

2. Throw beef, carrots, potatoes, onion and garlic in, add broth, Worcestershire, tomato paste paprika, thyme, rosemary, caraway seeds and bay leaves and stir. Season, cover and cook for 7 to 8 hrs on LOW OR on HIGH for 3 to 4 hrs

3. Whisk flour with ½ cup broth and add to slow cooker. Cover and cook for 30 mins more on HIGH until thickened.

CHICKEN MAIN DISHES

Chicken Casserole

Time: Up-to 7hrs 15 minutes | Serve 6

Ingredients:

♦ Butter

♦ ½tbsp olive oil

♦ 1½ tbsp flour

♦ 1 onion, chopped finely

♦ 650g (1.4lbs) chicken thigh fillets, boneless, skinless

♦ 400g (0.9 lbs) baby potatoes, halved

♦ 3 crushed garlic cloves

♦ 2 sticks celery, diced

♦ 2 carrots, diced

♦ 250g (9oz) mushrooms, quartered

♦ 500ml (17oz) chicken stock

♦ 15g (½-oz) dried porcini mushroom, soaked in 50ml (1.7oz) boiling water

♦ 2 tsp Dijon mustard, plus for serving

♦ 2 bay leaves

Preparation:

1. Caramelise onion in knob of butter and olive oil for 8 to 10 min in large frying pan. Meanwhile in separate bowl, toss chicken thighs in seasoned flour

2. Add garlic and chicken to pan and cook for 4 to 5 mins

3. Transfer to slow cooker. Add mushrooms, potatoes, celery, carrots, porcini mushrooms, soaking liquid, Dijon mustard, chicken stock, and bay leaves. Stir and cook on LOW for 7 hrs OR for 4hrs on HIGH.

Garlic-Parmesan Chicken

Time: 4 hrs15 minutes | Serves 4

Ingredients:

♦ 900g (2 lb) chicken thighs

♦ 3 tbsp extra-virgin olive oil

♦ Salt and ground black pepper

♦ 450g (1 lb) quartered baby potatoes

♦ 2 tbsp softened butter

♦ 2 tbsp fresh thyme

♦ 5 chopped cloves garlic

♦ 2 tbsp Parmesan freshly grated plus some for serving

♦ Freshly chopped parsley

Preparation:

1. Sear seasoned chicken in 1 tbsp hot oil for 3 mins per side

2. Coat potatoes in 2 tbsp oil, butter, salt and pepper, parsley, garlic, thyme, and Parmesan. Add chicken to this in slow cooker and cook on LOW for 8 hrs OR on HIGH for 4 hrs

3. Served garnished with Parmesan.

Pulled Chicken

Time: 6 hrs 15 minutes | Serves 6 to 10

Ingredients:

- 2 tbsp vegetable oil
- 10 to 12 chicken thighs, boneless, skinless
- 2 red onions, halved and sliced
- 2 crushed garlic cloves
- 2 tsp paprika
- 2 tbsp chipotle paste
- 250ml (8½-oz) passata
- 100g (3½-oz) barbecue sauce
- 1 tbsp light brown soft sugar
- 1 lime, juiced
- To serve (optional):
- burger buns/ taco shells/ guacamole/ potatoes/rice/ coriander leaves

Preparation:

1. Brown chicken in batches in a pan, relocating to slow cooker when browned. Once done, fry onions in remaining oil in same pan until just softened, approx. 5 mins. Add garlic and paprika and cook for a min. Empty into slow cooker. Deglaze with 100ml (3.3oz) water and add to cooker

2. Add chipotle paste, passata, barbecue sauce, sugar and lime juice. Season, stir, cover and cook for 6 to 8 hrs

3. Shred chicken with two forks through the sauce. Serve as preferred.

SEAFOOD AND FISH MAIN DISHES

Shrimp & Cheese Grits

Time: 6hrs 15 minutes | Serves 4

Ingredients:

♦ 2 or so cups grits

♦ ¼ cup cream

♦ 2 tbsp unsalted butter

♦ 1 cup grated cheese

♦ 2 tsp hot sauce

♦ 450g (1 lb) shrimp, deveined, cooked, peeled

♦ 1 tbsp Chives

♦ salt and pepper

Preparation:

1. Whisk together grits, salt and 8 cups water in slow cooker. Cover and cook on LOW until liquid is absorbed, 6 hrs. Add butter, cream cheese, hot sauce and stir to melt cheese

2. Top with raw shrimp. Cover and cook to warm shrimp through, approx. 5 mins

3. To serve, sprinkle with chives.

Seafood Stew

Time: 5hrs 5 minutes | Serves 8

Preparation:

1. Combine onions, celery, garlic, tomatoes, clam juice, tomato paste, wine, vinegar, oil, Italian seasoning, sugar, pepper flakes and bay leaf in slow cooker. Cover and cook for 4hrs on HIGH

2. Add fish, shrimp, clam juice, clams, and crabmeat. Cover and cook for 30 to 45 mins on LOW. Serve.

Ingredients:

♦ 1 cup finely chopped celery stalks
♦ 2 cups chopped onions
♦ 5 garlic cloves, grated
♦ 793g can (28-oz) diced tomatoes, undrained
♦ 225g bottle (8-oz) clam juice
♦ 170g can (6-oz) tomato paste
♦ 1 tbsp red wine vinegar
♦ ½ cup dry white wine/water
♦ 1 tbsp olive oil | 2½ tsp Italian seasoning
♦ ¼ tsp sugar | 1 bay leaf
♦ ¼ tsp crushed red pepper flakes
♦ 450g (1 lb) white fish, in 2½ cm (1-inch) pieces
♦ 340g (¾-lb) shrimp, raw, shelled deveined, tails removed
♦ 185g can (6½-oz.) chopped clams & juice, undrained
♦ 170g can (6-oz) crabmeat, drained
♦ ¼ cup fresh parsley, chopped

Paleo Moqueca (Brazilian Fish Stew)

Time: 4hrs15 minutes | Serves 2

Ingredients:

- 1 White Fish
- 1 tbsp Garlic Puree
- 250 ml Coconut Milk
- 1 diced Red Pepper
- 3 tbsp Coriander
- 1 tsp Rosemary
- 1 tbsp Paprika

- For the Sauce:
- 750ml (25oz) homemade tomato sauce
- 5 peeled carrots
- 1 baby marrow | 3 tomatoes
- 1 tsp Garlic Puree | 1 tsp Coriander
- 1 tsp Thyme | Salt & Pepper

Preparation:

1. Cut the vegetables into chunks and place in slow cooker (tomatoes, baby marrow and carrots). Stir in tomato sauce, garlic puree, coriander, thyme, and seasoning. Cook on LOW for 2 hrs

2. Add fish seasoned with salt, pepper and remaining garlic puree. Cook for 1 hour on LOW, until fish is ¾ cooked

3. Drain excess tomato sauce and stir in coconut milk, season, and add red pepper. Cook on LOW for 1 hour. Serve.

Shrimp Boil

Time: 8hrs 10 minutes | Serves 8

Ingredients:

- 900g (2 lbs) new potatoes, bite-size
- 4 cups stock/ chicken broth
- 450g (1 lb) andouille/kielbasa sausage in 2½-cm (1-inch) pieces
- 4 corn ears, husked, quartered
- 2 tbsp Old Bay seasoning
- ½ tsp cayenne pepper
- 900g (2 lbs) large shrimp, with tails
- 2 tbsp chopped parsley
- 4 tbsp melted butter
- Optional:
- cocktail dipping sauce
- lemon wedges

Preparation:

1. Place potatoes and chicken broth in cooker and top with sausage. Sprinkle with Old Bay seasoning and cayenne and add corn quarters. Cover and cook for 7 to 8hrs on LOW, OR on HIGH for 3 to 4 hrs

2. Turn slow cooker up to HIGH, gently add shrimp. Stir in, cover and cook for 10 min until shrimp are opaque. Relocate shrimp to serving dish using a slotted spoon and drizzle with cooking liquid

3. Mix melted butter with parsley , drizzle over top and toss. Serve with lemon wedges and cocktail sauce.

Coconut Seabass Curry

Time:1hr40 minutes | Serves 6

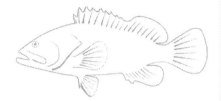

Ingredients:

- 1 tbs canola oil
- 2 finely chopped tomatoes, seeded
- 1 onion, finely chopped
- 1 tbs peeled and grated fresh ginger
- 3 tbs tamarind chutney
- ½ tsp ground turmeric
- 1 tsp ground coriander
- 1 tsp ancho
- 1 tsp yellow mustard seeds
- 425ml can (14 fl. oz) coconut milk, shaken
- 900g (2 lb) skinless thick sea bass, halibut or cod fillet, in 4cm (1 1/2-inch) pieces
- Garnish with cilantro leaves

Preparation:

1. Fry onion in oil and salt, stirring occasionally for 6 mins. Add tomatoes, chutney, ginger, coriander, ancho, mustard seeds, turmeric and salt. Stir while cooking for 5 mins, until tomatoes break down and spices become fragrant

2. Pour into slow cooker and stir in coconut milk. Cover and cook for 1 hour on LOW. Add fish, stirring to coat. Cover and cook on LOW for 30 mins until opaque. Serve.

VEGAN AND VEGETARIAN MAIN DISHES

Cauliflower and Potato Curry

Time: 5 hrs 10 minutes | Serves 6

Ingredients:

- ¼ to ⅓ cup Thai Red curry paste
- 1 tbs pomegranate/regular molasses
- 1 cauliflower, cut into florets
- 2 x 395g cans (14 oz) coconut milk
- 2 cups veggie broth
- 2 tbsp soy sauce
- 450g (1lb) baby potatoes, halved
- 1 cinnamon stick
- ½ tsp cumin seeds
- 2 cups fresh spinach
- Salt & pepper
- To serve:
- steamed rice, cilantro, limes, fresh naan

Preparation:

1. Combine curry paste, soy sauce, coconut milk, broth, and molasses in slow cooker and add cauliflower, potatoes, cinnamon, and cumin. Season lightly, cover and cook for 5 to 6 hrs on LOW OR on HIGH for 3 to 4 hrs

2. Stir spinach into curry mixture, cover and cook for 5 mins, until wilted

3. Top with lime and cilantro and serve with rice and fresh naan.

Vegetable Curry with Chickpeas

Time: 8 hrs 10 minutes | Serves 4

Ingredients:

- ♦ 4 cups cauliflower florets
- ♦ 1 peeled sweet potato, diced
- ♦ 2 cups Brussels sprouts, quartered
- ♦ 1 diced onion
- ♦ 1 diced red pepper
- ♦ 425g can (15 oz) chickpeas, drained
- ♦ 425g can (15oz) tomato sauce
- ♦ ½cup chicken/vegetable broth
- ♦ ½ cup coconut milk
- ♦ 1 tbsp cumin
- ♦ 1 tbsp turmeric
- ♦ 1 tbsp curry powder
- ♦ ½ tsp cayenne (optional)
- ♦ ½ cup frozen green peas
- ♦ salt and pepper
- ♦ Plain yogurt cilantro, sriracha and scallions

Preparation:

1. Cook vegetables, chickpeas, tomato sauce, coconut milk, chicken broth and spices on LOW for 8 hrs OR on HIGH for 4 hrs
2. Stir in green peas to warm, adjust seasoning
3. Serve with yogurt, cilantro and scallions, with accompaniment of choice.

Madras Lentils

Time: 4 hrs 10 minutes | Serves 6

Ingredients:

- 2 cups cooked lentils
- 1½ cups finely diced onion
- 2 cups canned tomato sauce/puree
- 2 to 3 cups potato, peeled and cubed
- 3 tbsp butter
- ½ cup unsweetened coconut milk
- ½ tsp cumin
- 3 cloves grated garlic
- ½ tsp dried oregano
- Salt & freshly ground black pepper crushed red pepper flakes

Preparation:

1. Toss all ingredients in lightly greased cooker. Cook on HIGH for 3½ to 4 hrs
2. Season and serve with accompaniments.

Butternut Squash Chili

Time: 4 hrs 15 minutes | Serves 8

Ingredients:

For the Chili:

- 680g (1½ lbs) peeled butternut, in 1 to 2cm (½ inch) pieces
- 1 can black beans
- 2 ½ cups chicken/vegetable broth
- 1 can great northern beans
- 1 each diced green and red bell pepper
- 1 diced sweet onion
- 1 can petite diced tomatoes
- 2 tsp chili powder
- ½ tsp ground ginger
- 5 grated cloves garlic
- 1 tsp ground cumin

Toppings:

- Cilantro, Sour Cream, Chips, Cheese

Preparation:

1. Cook all chili ingredients in slow cooker on LOW for 4 to 5 hrs, until butternut is tender

2. Serve with toppings.

Sweet Potato

Time: 4 hrs 5 minutes | Serves 5

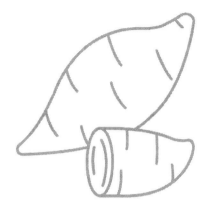

Ingredients:

♦ 5 sweet potatoes

Preparation:

1. Cook sweet potatoes on LOW for 5 to 7 hrs OR on HIGHT for 3 to 4 hrs, until soft.

2. Serve with your choice of toppings.

Masala Lentils

Time: 6 hrs 10 minutes | Serves 6 to 8

Ingredients:

- ♦ 3 cloves garlic, grated
- ♦ 1 chopped onion
- ♦ 1 tbsp grated fresh ginger OR 1 tsp ground ginger
- ♦ 4 cups vegetable broth
- ♦ 2¼ cups brown lentils
- ♦ 425g can (15 oz) diced tomatoes with juices
- ♦ ¼ cup tomato paste
- ♦ 1 tsp maple syrup
- ♦ ¾ tsp salt
- ♦ 2 tsp tamarind paste (optional)
- ♦ 1½ tsp garam masala
- ♦ 1 cup coconut milk
- ♦ black pepper
- ♦ For serving: Rice, quinoa, fresh herbs

Preparation:

1. Cook all ingredients except coconut milk in slow cooker on LOW for 6 hrs OR on HIGH for 3 to 4 hrs. Check for liquid content during last hour or two, and add more broth or water if needed

2. Stir in coconut milk as soon as lentils are cooked. Serve as preferred with fresh herb garnishing.

Thai Pine Vegetarian Curry

Time: 6 to 8 hrs | Serves 6

Ingredients:

- ◆ 1 can coconut milk
- ◆ 3 tbsp curry powder
- ◆ 1 tsp crushed red pepper
- ◆ 1½ tsp garlic salt
- ◆ 450g (1 lb) peeled sweet potatoes, in 2cm (1 inch) pieces
- ◆ 1 pineapple, cut in 2cm (1 inch) pieces
- ◆ 2 green bell peppers, in 2cm (1 inch) pieces
- ◆ 3 to 4 cups beans
- ◆ 2 onions, cut into 2cm (1 inch) pieces
- ◆ 1½ tsp salt
- ◆ To serve: Cooked rice
- ◆ Optional: Cashews, cilantro for topping

Preparation:

1. Whisk coconut milk, garlic, curry powder, salt, and crushed red pepper together in slow cooker and add remaining ingredients. Cook on LOW for 6 to 8 hrs OR on HIGH for 3 to 4 hrs

2. Serve garnished with cilantro.

VEGTABLE MAIN DISHES

Vegetable Lasagne

Time: 3 hours | Serves 4

Ingredients:

- 1 tbsp rapeseed oil
- 2 sliced onions
- 2 chopped garlic cloves
- 400g diced baby marrows (14oz)
- 1 red and 1 yellow pepper, deseeded, sliced roughly
- 400g can (14 oz) chopped tomatoes
- 2 tsp vegetable stock
- 2 tbsp tomato purée
- 15g (½-oz) chopped fresh basil, plus some leaves
- 1 aubergine, sliced length-wise
- 6 whole-wheat lasagne sheets
- ½ cup chopped buffalo mozzarella

Preparation:

1. Fry garlic and onions in rapeseed oil for 5 mins, stirring until soft. Add baby marrows, both peppers, chopped tomatoes, tomato purée, vegetable stock and chopped basil. Stir, cover and cook for 5 mins

2. Arrange aubergine slices in bottom of slow cooker dish, layered with 3 sheets of lasagne and then ⅓ of the ratatouille mixture, followed by remaining aubergine slices, last 3 lasagne sheet and ratatouille mixture. Cover and cook for 2½ to 3 hrs on HIGH

3. Dot with mozzarella, cover and allow 10 mins for the cheese to melt, sprinkle with extra basil and serve.

Veg Curry

Time: 6 hrs 10 minutes | Serves 4

Ingredients:

♦ 400ml can (13½-oz) coconut milk
♦ 3 tbsp mild curry paste
♦ 2 tsp vegetable stock powder
♦ 1 sliced red chilli, deseeded
♦ 1 tbsp finely chopped ginger
♦ 3 sliced garlic cloves
♦ 200g (7oz) chunks of butternut
♦ 1 sliced red pepper, deseeded
♦ 250g (9oz) thickly sliced aubergine, halved
♦ 15g (½-oz) coriander, chopped
♦ 160g (5.6oz) frozen peas, defrosted
♦ 1 lime, juiced
♦ flatbread

Preparation:

1. Combine coconut milk, curry paste, vegetable stock powder, red chilli, ginger, garlic cloves, butternut, red pepper and aubergine slices in slow cooker. Cover and refrigerate overnight

2. The following day cook on LOW for 6 hrs until tender. Stir in chopped coriander and defrosted peas and warm through. Add lime juice to taste.

Italian style Vegetable Bake

Time: 6 hrs 10 minutes | Serves 4

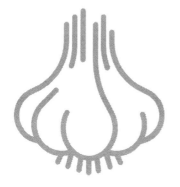

Ingredients:

- 3 crushed garlic cloves,
- 400g (14oz) can chopped tomato
- Chopped oregano leaves
- 1 whole garlic clove
- chilli flakes
- 300g (11oz) sliced baby/normal aubergines
- 2 sliced baby marrows
- 3 sliced tomatoes
- ½ large jar roasted red peppers
- torn basil, and some whole for sprinkling baguette, sliced and toasted
- 2 x 125g (4½ oz) torn balls mozzarella

Preparation:

1. Cook garlic, canned tomatoes, half the oregano leaves, chilli and seasoning on HIGH in slow cooker while preparing the vegetables. Tip out the sauce. Layer half the veg, herbs and seasoning (aubergines, baby marrows, red peppers, basil, tomatoes, and remaining oregano), then half bread rubbed with garlic clove, half mozzarella and half tipped-out tomato sauce. Repeat with veg, herb and tomato sauce layers, bread and mozzarella. Compress well and cook on HIGH for 5 to 6 hrs

2. To serve brown under grill to get a bubbling, golden finish and top with basil leaves.

Broccoli

Time: up to 4 hours | Serves 10

Ingredients:

♦ 6 cups chopped broccoli, partially thawed

♦ 304g can (10-¾ oz) undiluted condensed cream of celery soup,

♦ ¼ cup chopped onion

♦ 1½ cups grated cheddar cheese

♦ ½ tsp Worcestershire sauce

♦ ¼ tsp pepper

♦ 1 cup butter-flavoured crackers, crushed

♦ 2 tbsp butter

Preparation:

1. Combine broccoli, soup, 1 cup cheese, onion, Worcestershire sauce. Pour into greased slow cooker, sprinkling crushed crackers over the top and dotting with butter

2. Cover and cook on HIGH for 2-½to 3 hrs. Sprinkle with remaining cheese. Cook until melted.

RECIPES FOR SOUPS, STEWS AND CHILLI

Parsnip & Split Pea Soup

Time: 1 to 8 hrs | Serves 4 to 6

Ingredients:

- 1 tbsp olive oil or ¼ cup water
- 1 diced onion
- 2 or 3 garlic cloves, grated
- 2 chopped parsnips
- 2 chopped carrots
- 453 g (1 lb) dried green split peas, rinsed
- 1 tsp dried thyme
- 1 tsp chicken seasoning
- 2 bay leaves
- 6 cups vegetable broth/water, or more
- 1 tsp liquid smoke, optional
- Salt & freshly cracked pepper to taste

Preparation:

1. Sauté onions, garlic, carrots and parsnips in olive oil until onions are translucent, around 4 mins, and place in slow cooker. Add remaining ingredients and cook on LOW for 8 hrs. Remove bay leaves, blend to preferred consistency and add seasoning to taste.

Lentil Tortilla Soup

Time: 50 minutes | Serves 6

Preparation:

1. Cook bell pepper, jalapeño, corn, lentils, black beans, pinto beans, broth, tomato sauce, tomato paste, salsa verde, herbs and spices in cooker on LOW for 7 to 8 hrs OR for 4 to 6 hours on HIGH

2. Mix in cream and serve with preferred toppings.

Ingredients:

- ♦ 1 tsp olive/avocado oil
- ♦ 1 cup onion, diced
- ♦ 1 diced jalapeno pepper | 1 diced bell pepper
- ♦ 2 ½ cups vegetable/chicken broth
- ♦ 425g can (15 oz) crushed tomatoes/ tomato sauce
- ♦ ½ cup salsa | 1 tbsp tomato paste
- ♦ 425g can (15 oz) drained & rinsed black beans
- ♦ 425g can (15 oz) pinto beans | ¾ cup dried red lentils
- ♦ 1 cup corn | ½ tsp chili powder | ½ tsp cumin
- ♦ ½tsp garlic powder | ¼ to ½ cup cream (optional)
- ♦ ¼ tsp cayenne pepper | salt and pepper

Toppings:
- ♦ crushed tortilla chips | shredded cheese
- ♦ jalapeños, sliced or diced | red onion, chopped
- ♦ pico de gallo | avocado, sliced
- ♦ cilantro | sour cream/ Greek yogurt

Chicken Soup

Time: 4 hrs 15 minutes | Serves 4

Ingredients:

- 6 cups chicken stock
- 2 tbsp extra virgin olive oil
- 2 tbsp butter
- 2 onions, chopped
- 2 leeks, chopped | 2 ribs celery, chopped
- 2 parsnips, chopped | 4 carrots, chopped
- 8 peppercorns
- 1 bay leaf | 2 sprigs fresh rosemary
- 4 sprigs fresh thyme
- 900g – 1.3kg (2-3 lbs) chicken breasts/thighs
- 1 lemon, juice and zest | Salt and black pepper
- ¾ cup dry farro
- ½ cup cilantro/ mixed herbs

Preparation:

1. Combine chicken stock, butter, olive oil, onions, carrots, parsnips, celery, leeks, peppercorns, thyme, rosemary, bay leaf, and a pinch of salt and pepper. Add chicken, cover and cook for 5 to 6hrs on LOW OR on HIGH for 4 to 5 hrs

2. Remove chicken about 45 mins before serving. Shred it and discard the herbs. Stir in farro, lemon juice and zest. Stir the shredded chicken into soup and cook until the farro is tender.

Moroccan Chickpea Stew

Time: 4 hrs 10 minutes | Serves 6

Ingredients:

- 1 chopped onion
- 3 grated garlic cloves
- 1 peeled butternut, in bite sized pieces
- 1 chopped red bell pepper
- ¾ cup red lentils
- 425g can (15 oz)chickpeas
- 425g can (15 oz) pure tomato sauce
- 1 tsp grated ginger
- 1 tsp turmeric | 1 tsp cumin
- ½ tsp cinnamon | 1 tsp smoked paprika
- salt and pepper | 3 cups veg broth

To serve:

- cooked quinoa | arugula
- coconut yogurt

Preparation:

1. Stir all ingredients in slow cooker, cover and cook on LOW for 6 to 7 hrs OR on HIGH for 3 to 4 hrs

2. To thicken, remove lid for last 1 hour of cooking to reduce

3. Serve with a handful of arugula, quinoa and a dollop of yogurt.

Beef Stew

Time: 8 hrs 50 minutes | Serves 8

Ingredients:

- 2 tbsp olive oil
- 453g (1 lb) baby red potatoes, quartered
- 900g (2 lbs) 2 cm (1 inch) cubes stew meat
- 4 carrots, diagonally sliced to 1cm (½inch)
- 1 diced onion
- 3 grated garlic cloves
- 3 cups beef broth | 2 tbsp tomato paste
- 1 tbsp Worcestershire sauce
- 1 tsp caraway seeds (optional)
- 1 tsp dried thyme | 1 tsp dried rosemary
- 1 tsp smoked paprika
- 2 bay leaves | ¼ cup flour
- 2 tbsp parsley leaves, chopped
- Salt and freshly ground black pepper

Preparation:

1. Season beef and brown evenly in heated olive oil for 2 to3 mins

2. Cook beef, potatoes, onion, carrots, garlic, beef broth, tomato paste, Worcestershire, thyme, rosemary, paprika, caraway seeds bay leaves and seasoning, covered on LOW for 7 to 8 hrs OR on HIGH for 3 to 4 hrs.

3. Whisk flour and ½ cup stew broth together and stir mixture into slow cooker. Cover and cook on HIGH for 30 mins, until thickened

4. Serve immediately, with parsley.

Chilli

Time: 6 hrs 25 minutes | Serves 4 to 6

Ingredients:

- 1 tbsp olive oil | 900g (2 lbs) lean minced beef

- 3 grated cloves of garlic | 1 finely chopped onion

- 2 x 411g cans (14.5 oz) diced tomatoes with green chilies

- ½ cup beef broth

- 3 x 227g (8 oz) cans tomato sauce

- 2 tsp cocoa powder

- ½ tsp ground coriander | 2 tbsp chili powder

- 2 tsp paprika | 2 ½ tsp ground cumin

- 1 tsp granulated sugar

- Salt and freshly ground black pepper

- 425g can (15 oz) drained and rinsed dark red kidney beans

- 425g can (15 oz) drained and rinsed light red kidney beans

To serve:

- Grated cheddar cheese

Preparation:

1. Using a deep non-stick pan, sauté onions in olive oil for 3 mins, add garlic and sauté for 30 seconds. Pour onion mix into slow cooker.

2. Brown beef, stirring occasionally. Drain fat, leaving 2 tbsp of fat and relocate beef to slow cooker. Stir in beef broth, tomato sauce, tomatoes, chili powder, cumin, paprika, cocoa powder, sugar, coriander. Season to taste. Cover and cook on LOW for 5 to 6 hrs

3. Stir in dark and light red kidney beans and heat through for about 2 mins. Serve with toppings.

Lentil & Quinoa Chilli

Time: 4 hrs 10 minutes | Serves 8

Ingredients:

- 1 chopped onion
- 3 grated garlic cloves
- 2 chopped bell peppers
- 1 chopped celery stalk
- 425g can (15 oz)diced tomatoes
- 1 cup water
- 4 cups vegetable broth
- 1 cup dried lentils
- 425g can (15 oz) Pinto Beans
- 2 tbsp chili powder
- 1 tbsp oregano
- 2 tsp cumin
- ½ cup uncooked quinoa
- Salt

Preparation:

1. Cook all ingredients in slow cooker on LOW for 8 hours OR on HIGH for 4 hours

2. Serve with preferred toppings, such as shredded cheese, plain Greek yogurt or sour cream, avocado, green onion, and cilantro.

RECIPES FOR DESSERTS

Peanut Butter Chocolate Cake

Time: 2 hrs 15 minutes | Serves 10

Ingredients:

- 430g (15.25 oz) devil's food cake mix
- 1 cup water
- ½ cup salted butter. melted
- 3 eggs
- 227g (8oz) mini Reese peanut butter cups

For the topping:

- 3 tbsp icing sugar
- 1 cup smooth peanut butter
- 10 Reese's peanut butter cups

Preparation:

1. Mix cake mix, water, butter, and eggs until smooth, and add the mini peanut butter cups

2. Line slow cooker dish with non-stick spray and add the batter, spreading it evenly. Cover and cook on HIGH for 2 hrs without removing lid until done. Remove from heat

3. Set on stove top and add peanut butter, stirring until smooth and melted. Add icing sugar and whisk until smooth. Pour peanut butter melt over the warm cake and top with peanut butter cups.

Choc Chip Cookie Bars

Time: 3hrs 5 minutes | Makes 16

Ingredients:

♦ 1 cup salted butter, melted

♦ 3 tsp vanilla extract

♦ 2 large eggs

♦ 2 cups brown sugar, tightly packed

♦ 2 cups flour

♦ Salt

♦ 1 cup chocolate chips

Preparation:

1. Create a foil bowl, lining slow cooker with aluminium foil

2. Smooth together melted butter and brown sugar, add vanilla extract and eggs and stir again until smooth. Stir in salt and flour

3. Pour batter into the foil lined cooker and sprinkle chocolate chips on top. Place paper towel under cooker the lid and cook for 2½ to 3 hrs on HIGH until the middle is set. Remove using the aluminium foil and cool for 1 hour minimum before cutting and serving.

Hot Fudge Chocolate Cake

Time: 2hrs| Makes 6 to 8

Ingredients:

- 1 cup flour
- ½ cup sugar
- 1 tsp baking powder
- ¼ cup cocoa powder
- Salt
- ¾ cup milk
- ⅓ cup canola/ vegetable oil
- ½ cup sugar
- 1 tsp vanilla extract
- 1 cup chocolate chips
- 3 tbsp cocoa powder
- 1 ½ cups boiling water

Preparation:

1. Line the cooker dish or use non-stick cooking spray

2. Whisk flour, ½ cup sugar, cocoa powder, and baking powder to mix. Stir in milk, oil, and vanilla until moist. Pour into greased/lined slow cooker and spread evenly. Sprinkle with chocolate chips and set one side

3. Whisk ½ cup sugar, 3 tbsp cocoa powder and boiling water together in bowl and pour this hot mixture over the batter in slow cooker. Do not stir. Allow to turn into hot fudge as the cake bakes. Cover and cook on HIGH for 1½ to 2 hrs. Use the clean toothpick method to ensure it is baked through

4. Remove cooker dish from base and allow cake to cool before serving.

RECIPES FOR SNACKS

Buffalo Chicken Meatballs

Time: 2hrs 20 minutes | Makes 6 to 8

Ingredients:

- 450g (1 lb) ground chicken
- ¾ cup breadcrumbs
- 1 egg
- ½ tsp garlic powder
- ½ tsp onion powder
- 2 thinly sliced green onions
- ¾ cup buffalo sauce
- Salt and ground black pepper
- ¼ cup blue cheese dressing

Preparation:

1. Preheat oven to 200°C (400°F) Prepare baking sheet

2. Combine chicken, breadcrumbs, egg, garlic & onion powder, onions and seasoning, using wooden spoon/hands. Roll mixture into approx. 24 x 3 to 4 cm (1¼ - 1½ inch) meatballs

3. Bake meatballs on baking sheet for 4 to 5 mins, until cooked. Move to slow cooker, add buffalo sauce and gently combine, cover and cook on LOW for 2 hrs

4. Serve drizzled with blue cheese dressing.

Moroccan Chicken Pita Bites

Time: 1½ to 2hrs | Makes 6 to 8

Ingredients:

- 450g (1 lb) Boneless Chicken Thighs
- 1 sliced onion
- 1 tbsp grated Ginger
- 1 tbsp grated Garlic
- 2 tsp Ground Cumin
- 1 tsp Cinnamon
- 1 to 2 tbsp Paprika
- 1½ cups Chicken Stock
- 2 tbsp Lemon Juice
- ½ cup Green Olives quartered
- Salt to taste
- 3 tbsp oil | 5 to 6 Pita breads
- Hummus | Fresh Parsley

Preparation:

1. Sauté onions and salt and pepper add ginger and garlic and cook for a minute. Add cumin and cinnamon and combine. Cook for a few mins

2. Cover chicken thighs with onion mixture in slow cooker. Add 2 cups chicken stock, olives, lemon juice and salt and pepper, cover and cook on LOW for 6 to 7 hrs. Shred the chicken once cooked

3. Pre-heat oven to 175°C (350°F). Quarter the pitas, arrange on baking sheet and toast in oven until crispy, about 9 mins

4. Serve hot with hummus, about 1 tbsp of Moroccan chicken, garnished with parsley.

RECIPES FOR KETO MEALS

Carne Asada

Time: 8hrs 10 minutes | Serve 4

Ingredients:

- 2 chipotle peppers in adobo sauce
- 1 tbsp extra-virgin olive oil
- ½ cup freshly squeezed orange juice
- 4 garlic cloves
- 1 lime, juiced
- 1 tsp fish sauce
- ¼ cup cilantro, chopped
- ½ tsp paprika
- ½ tsp ground cumin
- ½ tsp salt
- 900g (2 lbs) steak

Preparation:

1. Blend all ingredients, except steak until smooth
2. Pan sear meat on both sides and move to slow cooker. Cover with sauce mixture and cook on LOW for 8 hrs
3. Shred the meat with two forks and serve over a salad, nachos, or in lettuce leaf tacos.

Lemon Pepper Pork Tenderloin

Time: 4hrs 10 minutes | Serve 6

Ingredients:

- 900g to 1.4kg (2-3 lbs) pork tenderloin
- 1 lemon, juiced
- 4 chopped garlic cloves
- 2 tbsp olive oil
- ½ to 1 tsp thickener for the gravy
- salt and pepper

Preparation:

1. Cook pork, garlic, olive oil, lemon juice, salt, and pepper, covered in slow cooker for 3 to 4 hrs on LOW. Remove and allow to rest

2. Add thickener to the cooking liquid and whisk it in, increasing slow cooker to HIGH, whisking occasionally until gravy thickens. Slice pork and serve with gravy.

Lamb with Mint & Green Beans

Time: 6 to 10 hrs | Serve 4

Ingredients:

- 1.5kg (3.3 lbs) leg of lamb, bone in
- 2 tbsp ghee
- 4 garlic cloves
- ¼ cup chopped mint/1-2 tbsp dried mint
- 600g (21 oz) trimmed green beans
- ½ tsp salt or more to taste
- ground black pepper

Preparation:

1. Pre-warm slow cooker. Pat lamb dry and season with salt and pepper

2. Grease pot with ghee, fry lamb until golden, turning to brown all sides

3. Move browned lamb to slow cooker and sprinkle with mint and garlic. If lamb dries, add ½ to 1 cup water. Cover and cook on LOW for 10 hrs OR on HIGH for 6 hrs. After 4 hours, remove lamb to a plate. Add green beans and lamb and cook for 2 hrs until the green beans are crisp.

Garlic-Herb Mashed Cauliflower

Serves 6

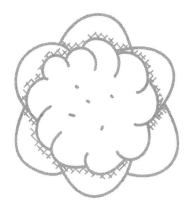

Ingredients:

- 1 cauliflower head, in bite-sizes
- 5 smashed garlic cloves
- 3 tbsp butter cubes
- 4 cups vegetable broth
- ⅓ cup Greek yogurt
- 1 tsp garlic powder
- 1 tbsp parsley, chopped
- 2 tbsp chives, chopped
- 1 tbsp rosemary, chopped
- Salt and freshly ground black pepper

Preparation:

1. Cover cauliflower and garlic in broth and cook about 2½ to 3 hrs on HIGH until the cauliflower is tender. Drain through a strainer, making sure to retain ½ cup of broth. Mash the cauliflower, add butter and yogurt, and mash until smooth

2. Mix in chives, garlic powder, parsley, rosemary and seasoning

3. Serve.

Mediterranean Frittata

Time: 3hrs 30 minutes | Serve 6

Ingredients:

- 8 eggs
- ⅓ cup milk
- 4 cups baby arugula
- 1 tsp dried oregano
- 1¼ cups roasted red peppers, chopped
- ½ cup red onion, thinly sliced
- ¾ cup goat cheese, crumbled
- Salt and freshly ground black pepper

Preparation:

1. Grease inside of slow cooker with non-stick spray
2. Whisk eggs, milk and oregano and season
3. Cook arugula, roasted red peppers, onion and goat cheese covered with egg mix on LOW for 2½ to 3 hrs
4. Serve immediately.

Thai Chicken Thighs

Time: 6hrs 5 minutes | Serve 4

Ingredients:

♦ 8 chicken thighs, boneless and skinless

♦ 1½ cups water

♦ 1 tsp grated ginger

♦ 1 tbsp sesame oil

♦ 1 - 2 tsp Sriracha sauce

♦ 3 tbsp peanut butter

♦ ½ tsp chili pepper flakes

♦ 3 tbsp tomato paste

♦ ½ cup coconut milk

♦ salt and pepper1 tbsp fish sauce

Preparation:

1. Wash chicken thighs and place in slow cooker

2. Mix remaining ingredients in bowl and whisk until smooth. Pour over chicken thighs ensuring chicken is covered. If not, add water. Cook on LOW for 5 to 6 hrs OR on HIGH for 4 hours

3. Serve over rice.

Spring Beef Bourguignon

Time: 6hrs 25 minutes | Serve 6

Ingredients:

- 1.8 kg (4 lb) beef chuck roast, cut into chunks
- 1 cup red wine
- 3 tbsp extra-virgin olive oil
- 1 cup beef broth
- 2 large sliced carrots
- 2 cups sliced baby mushrooms
- 2 chopped cloves of garlic
- 1 diced onion
- 3 sprigs rosemary
- 3 sprigs of thyme
- 1 bunch asparagus quartered
- Chopped parsley

Preparation:

1. Sear beef in batches for 3 mins on each side, deglazing between batches using red wine. Add deglazing and seared beef to slow cooker
2. Add beef broth, carrots, onion, mushrooms, garlic, thyme, rosemary and remaining red wine and cook on HIGH for 6 to 7 hrs, until beef is easy to shred. 30 mins before serving, take out herbs, add asparagus and cook until just tender
3. Serve garnished with parsley.

Zuppa Toscana Soup

Time: 4hrs 10 minutes | Serve 10

Ingredients:

- ♦ 450g (1 lb) mild/hot Italian sausage
- ♦ 1 tbsp oil
- ♦ ½ cup onion, finely diced
- ♦ 3grated garlic cloves
- ♦ 1.6 l (36 oz) chicken/vegetable stock
- ♦ 1 diced cauliflower head
- ♦ 3 cups chopped kale
- ♦ ¼ tsp red pepper flakes, crushed
- ♦ Salt and pepper
- ♦ ½ cup cream

Preparation:

1. Brown ground sausage, remove with slotted spoon to cook further in slow cooker. Discard the grease

2. Sauté onions in oil for 3 to 4 mins until translucent

3. Add onions, stock, cauliflower florets, kale, pepper flakes, salt, and pepper, mix well and cook on LOW for 8 hrs OR on HIGH 4 hrs. Add the cream

4. Serve.

Low Carb Chilli

Time: 8hrs 15 minutes | Makes 10 cups

Ingredients:

- 225g (½lb) Ground beef
- ½ Onion, chopped
- 8 grated Garlic cloves
- 2 x 425g cans (15 oz) Diced tomatoes, with liquid
- 170g can (6 oz) Tomato paste
- 113g can (4 oz) Green chillies, with liquid
- 2 tbsp Worcestershire sauce
- ¼ cup Chili powder
- 2 tbsp Cumin
- 1 tbsp Dried oregano
- 2 tsp Sea salt
- 1 tsp Black pepper
- 1 medium Bay leaf (optional)

Preparation:

1. Over medium heat cook onion for 5 to7 mins in pan, until translucent. Add garlic and cook for about 1 minute. Add beef and brown for 8 to 10 mins

2. Add beef and all ingredients, except bay leaf. Stir to combine. Place bay leaf in the middle. Cook for 6 to 8 hrs on LOW OR on HIGH for 3 to 4 hrs. Discard the bay leaf before serving.

Keto Broccoli Cheese

Time: 3hrs 10 minutes | Serves 12

Ingredients:

+ 2 cups water
+ 2 cups heated chicken broth
+ 5 cups broccoli florets, cut up
+ 225g (8 oz) softened cream cheese
+ 1 cup whipping cream
+ ½ cup Parmesan cheese
+ 2½ cups Cheddar cheese, shredded
+ 2 tbsp softened unsalted butter
+ thyme
+ Salt and pepper

Preparation:

1. Mix butter, softened cream cheese, whipping cream, chicken broth, and water in slow cooker. Add parmesan cheese, broccoli crowns and thyme. Cover and cook on LOW for 3 hours. Stir and add 2 ½ cups grated cheddar cheese, stirring to melt cheese completely. Season to taste

2. Serve hot.

RECIPES FOR
LOW CARB MEALS

Frittata with Kale, Roasted Red Pepper, and Feta

Time: 3hrs 20 minutes | Makes 8

Ingredients:

- Non-stick spray or oil
- 1 – 2 tsp olive oil to sauté kale
- 140g (5 oz) baby kale, washed & dried
- 170g (6 oz) diced roasted red pepper
- ¼ cup green onion, sliced
- 113-140g (4-5 oz) crumbled Feta
- 8 well beaten eggs
- ½ tsp all-purpose seasoning blend
- Black pepper
- Low fat sour cream for serving (optional)

Preparation:

1. Sauté kale in heated oil until softened

2. Move kale to slow cooker that has been prepared with non-stick spray or oil

3. Add red pepper and green onion. Pour beaten eggs over top, season and sprinkle with Feta. Cook on LOW for 2 to 3 hrs, until frittata is well set, and cheese is melted

4. Serve hot, with a dollop of sour cream.

Chicken Bacon Chowder

Time: | Serves 8

Ingredients:

- ◆ 4grated cloves garlic
- ◆ 1 cleaned, trimmed and sliced leek
- ◆ 1 finely chopped shallot
- ◆ 2 diced celery
- ◆ 170g (6 oz) sliced cremini mushrooms
- ◆ 1 onion sliced | 2 cups chicken stock,
- ◆ 4 tbsp butter | 450g (1lb) chicken breasts
- ◆ 225g (8 oz) cream cheese
- ◆ 450g (1 lb) crispy bacon, crumbled
- ◆ 1 cup cream | 1 tsp dried thyme
- ◆ Salt and pepper1 tsp garlic powder

Preparation:

1. Cook garlic, onions, celery, shallot, leek, mushrooms, 2 tbsp butter, 1 cup chicken stock, sea salt and black pepper on LOW, covered for 1 hr

2. Meanwhile brown both sides of chicken breasts in remaining 2 tbsp butter for about 5 mins each side

3. Remove chicken and put one side. Scrape chicken bits from pan and add to chicken stock in slow cooker. Add heavy cream, garlic powder, cream cheese, and thyme. Stir well. Add cooled chicken, cubed, and bacon to slow cooker. Stir until well mixed, cover and cook for 6 to 8 hrs

4. Serve.

Broccoli Cheese Soup

Time: 4hrs 20 minutes | Serve 10

Ingredients:

- ♦ 900g (32 oz) broccoli florets
- ♦ ½ diced onion
- ♦ 2 grated garlic cloves
- ♦ 2 cups cream
- ♦ 4 cups chicken broth
- ♦ 1 tsp ground mustard
- ♦ ¼ tsp red pepper flakes
- ♦ 4 cups cheddar, grated
- ♦ 1½ cups grated Monterey jack
- ♦ Salt and pepper

Preparation:

1. Cook broccoli, onion, garlic, chicken, ground mustard, broth, cream, red pepper flakes, salt, and pepper, covered, on LOW for 4 hrs, until broccoli is tender

2. Blend to smooth consistency. Add cheese and stir until melted and creamy

3. Serve immediately with crumbled bacon, if desired.

Cauliflower Bolognese with Zucchini Noodles

Time: 3 hrs 30 minutes | Serves 5 to 6

Ingredients:

For the Bolognese:

- Florets of 1 cauliflower
- ¾ cup onion, diced
- 1 tsp dried basil flakes
- 2 grated garlic cloves
- 2 tsp dried oregano flakes
- 2 x 400 g cans (14oz)diced tomatoes
- ½ cup low-sodium vegetable broth
- ¼tsp red pepper flakes
- salt and pepper

For the pasta:

- 5 zucchinis

Preparation:

1. Cook all Bolognese ingredients on HIGH for 3½ hours in slow cooker. When cooked, mash cauliflower to break up florets and create a "Bolognese"

2. Spread Bolognese over bowls of zucchini noodles to serve.

Buffalo Chicken Lettuce Wraps

Time: | Serves 6

Ingredients:

- ♦ 3 boneless skinless chicken breasts
- ♦ 1 celery stalk
- ♦ 1 diced onion
- ♦ 1 garlic clove
- ♦ 475ml (16 oz) low sodium chicken broth
- ♦ ½ cup hot wing sauce
- ♦ Lettuce leaves
- ♦ 1½ cups carrots, shredded
- ♦ 2 thinly sliced celery stalks
- ♦ To serve: blue cheese, ranch dressing

Preparation:

1. Cook chicken, onions, celery stalk, garlic, and broth, covered on LOW for 8 hrs OR on HIGH for 4 hrs. Remove chicken from pot, retain ½ cup broth, and discard the rest. Shred chicken with two forks and return to slow cooker with reserved broth and hot sauce. Cook on HIGH for 30 mins

2. Serve chicken in lettuce cups, with buffalo chicken, shredded carrots, chopped celery, blue cheese, and ranch dressing as topping.

Southwestern Pot Roast

Time: 4 to 5 hrs | Serves 6

Ingredients:

- 1.4kg (3 lbs)boneless chuck roast, fat-trimmed
- 415ml can (14 oz) low-sodium beef broth
- 1 ¼ cup preferred salsa
- Steak seasoning
- 1-2 tsp olive oil for browning

Preparation:

1. Simmer beef broth in small pan, removing fat from the top until broth is reduced to ½ cup. Remove all visible fat while reducing. Rub pot roast on all sides with steak seasoning

2. Brown roast in heated olive oil in heavy frying pan. Once browned on all sides, place in slow cooker in a single layer

3. Pour reduced broth into frying pan, deglazing caramelised bits. Stir salsa into broth and pour mixture over pot roast. Cook on HIGH for one hour, then a further 3 to 4 hrs on LOW, until meat is tender

4. Remove roast from slow cooker and pour sauce into a small pan. Return roast to slow cooker. To sauce, add ¼ cup salsa and simmer in pan to reduce to 1 cup

5. Serve with sauce.

Chicken Cacciatore

Time: 3 hrs 10 minutes | Serves 4

Ingredients:

- 2 grated cloves of Garlic
- ½ onion, diced
- 1 diced Red bell pepper
- 411g can (14.5 oz) diced tomatoes
- 4 Chicken breasts
- 1 tbsp each chopped thyme and rosemary
- Salt & Black pepper
- 1 Bay leaf

Preparation:

1. Season chicken breasts in slow cooker

2. Stir garlic, onion, bell peppers, diced tomatoes, thyme and rosemary together in a bowl. Pour evenly over chicken and place bay leaf in the centre. Cover and cook for 6 to 8 hrs on LOW OR for 3 to 4 hrs on HIGH

3. Serve hot.

Poached Salmon

Time: | Serves 4 to 6

Ingredients:

- 1 cup dry white wine
- 2 cups water
- 1 thinly sliced lemon
- 1 thinly sliced shallot
- 5 to 6 sprigs of tarragon, dill, and/or Italian parsley
- 1 bay leaf
- 1 tsp black peppercorns and salt
- 900g (2 lbs) OR 4-6 fillets of salmon with skin
- salt and freshly ground black pepper
- Serve: Lemon wedges, coarse sea salt, and olive oil

Preparation:

1. Cook wine, water, lemon, shallots, peppercorns, bay leaf, herbs, and salt on HIGH for 30 mins

2. Season top of salmon and place skin side down in slow cooker,. Cover and cook on LOW until salmon becomes opaque and flakes easily. Monitor 45 mins into cooking until cooked as desired

3. Drizzle with olive oil to serve and sprinkle with coarse salt and lemon wedges.

Lemon-Garlic Chicken Breast

Time: | Serves 4

Ingredients:

♦ 4 boneless, skinless chicken breasts

♦ 1 tbsp olive oil

♦ 1 cup chicken broth

♦ 8 cloves crushed garlic

♦ ½ cup freshly squeezed lemon juice

♦ 2 tbsp unsalted butter

♦ 2 tbsp flour

♦ Salt and pepper

♦ parsley leaves, chopped (optional)

Preparation:

1. Generously season chicken breasts and brown in heated oil for about 5 mins. Move to slow cooked with brown side up in one layer at bottom and add broth, garlic and lemon juice. Cover and cook on LOW for 3 to 4 hrs. Meanwhile, finger rub the flour into butter and set aside

2. Plate the chicken but retain the cooking liquid. Bring liquid to boil in pan. Add butter mixture and whisk into the sauce. Cook, stirring, for 3 to 4 mins until sauce thickens

3. To serve, pour over the chicken, sprinkle with parsley

Pork Vindaloo

Time: | Serves 6 to 8

Ingredients:

- 9 cm (3½ inch) peeled ginger | 3 tbsp canola oil
- 1.8 kg (4 lbs) pork shoulder, quartered to 5cm (1 ½ - 2 inch) cubes
- 3 thinly sliced onions | ½tsp fenugreek seeds
- 10 to 12 cloves grated garlic | 3 to 6 grated serrano chillies
- 1½ - 2½ tsp ground Indian red chilli
- ½ tsp turmeric | 2 tbsp coriander seeds
- ½ tsp whole brown mustard seeds
- 1 tsp cumin seeds | 4 to 6 cloves
- 20 black peppercorns | 3 - 4 black cardamom pods
- 2½ cm (1 inch) piece cassia | 1 tsp sugar
- 2 tbsp tamarind paste | 1 tbsp white vinegar | salt

Preparation:

1. Warm inner bowl by heating slow cooker on HIGH for 15 mins. Julienne 2½ cm of ginger to use for garnish.

2. Grate the remaining ginger

3. In heated oil over high heat, add fenugreek seeds, covering immediately to avoid splattering. Add onions once seeds stop sputtering. Sauté onions for 7 - 8 mins until golden-brown. Add to slow cooker with pork, grated ginger, garlic, serrano chillies, turmeric, ground red chilli, and salt and cook on LOW for 3 ½ hrs

4. Grind coriander seeds, cumin seeds, mustard seeds, cloves, cardamom, peppercorns, cassia, and sugar together using spice grinder. Add to the pork, mix well. Cook on LOW for 30 mins. Turn off slow cooker and stir in tamarind pulp and vinegar. Serve garnished with julienned ginger.

Disclaimer

The opinions and ideas of the author contained in this publication are designed to educate the reader in an informative and helpful manner. While we accept that the instructions will not suit every reader, it is only to be expected that the recipes might not gel with everyone. Use the book responsibly and at your own risk. This work with all its contents, does not guarantee correctness, completion, quality or correctness of the provided information. Always check with your medical practitioner should you be unsure whether to follow a low carb eating plan. Misinformation or misprints cannot be completely eliminated. Human error is real!

Photo: Larisa Blinova // www.shutterstock.com

Design: Olviiaprodesign // www.fiverr.com

Printed in Great
Britain
by Amazon